HUGE Earthmovers

by Meish Goldish

Consultant: James Acock
Heavy Vehicle Specialist
D & A Consultants, Inc.

BEARPORT
PUBLISHING

New York, New York

Credits

Cover and Title Page, © Elemental Imaging/Shutterstock; TOC, © Buhantsov Alexey/Shutterstock; 4, Courtesy of Caterpillar Inc.; 5, © Darren Jensen; 6, © Eric Orlemann/LeTourneau Technologies; 7, © Eric Orlemann/LeTourneau Technologies; 8, © 2007 by Karen Carr and Karen Carr Studio; Inc.; 9, Courtesy of Terex Mining Corp.; 10, © David Troy/Alamy; 11T, © Tim Twichell; 11B, © Tim Twichell; 12, © Martin Röll; 13, © AP Images/Frank Augstein; 14, © Michael Gaar/Marketing Communications/Atlas Copco; 15, © Heinz Meinert/Marketing Communications/Atlas Copco; 16, © AP Images/EyePress; 17, © Erwin Fleischmann/Herrenknecht; 18, © Anke Van Wyk/Shutterstock; 19, Courtesy of Hydraulics & Pneumatics Magazine, Penton Media Inc.; 20-21, © Jan De Nul NV; 22T, © David Scheuber/iStockphoto; 22TL, © Ralf Broskvar/iStockphoto; 22TR, © David Freund/iStockphoto; 22BL, © Christian Lagerek/Shutterstock; 22BR, © asterix0597/iStockphoto; 22A, © Jan De Nul NV; 22B, © Joan Gravell/Alamy; 22C, © Mikhail Lavrenov/Shutterstock; 22D, © Bato/Shutterstock; 22E, © AraBus/Shutterstock; 22F, © Maxim Shipenkov/ITAR-TASS/Landov; 22G, © Julio de la Higuera Rodrigo/iStockphoto; 22H, © Erwin Fleischmann/Herrenknecht.

Publisher: Kenn Goin
Editorial Director: Adam Siegel
Creative Director: Spencer Brinker
Photo Researcher: Omni-Photo Communications, Inc.
Design: Debrah Kaiser

Library of Congress Cataloging-in-Publication Data

Goldish, Meish.
  Huge earthmovers / by Meish Goldish.
    p. cm. — (World's biggest)
  Includes bibliographical references and index.
  ISBN-13: 978-1-59716-955-4 (library binding)
  ISBN-10: 1-59716-955-2 (library binding)
  1. Earthmoving machinery—Juvenile literature. I. Title.

TA725.G627 2010
624.1'52—dc22
                          2009011776

For more information, write to Bearport Publishing Company, Inc., 101 Fifth Avenue, Suite 6R, New York, New York 10003. Printed in the United States of America.

10 9 8 7 6 5 4 3 2 1

CONTENTS

DUMP TRUCK

Caterpillar 797B

Length: 47 feet, 6 inches (14.5 m)

Width: 32 feet (9.8 m)

Height: 23 feet, 1 inch (7 m); with bed tilted, 50 feet, 2 inches (15.3 m)

Weight: 306.8 tons (278 metric tons)

Huge earthmovers are used at building and **mine** sites. They dig up and move tons of dirt, rocks, and sand. Some of these machines are so big that they can't even be driven on streets or highways. Instead, they are shipped in pieces from the factory to their work areas, where they are then put together.

The Caterpillar 797B is a giant **dump truck** that can carry away up to 380 tons (345 metric tons) of thick, oily sand dug from a mine. The truck is taller than a two-story building. Its height doubles when the back of the dump truck, called a bed, is tilted to dump its load. Even the truck's six tires are huge. Each one is about 13 feet (4 m) high. That's taller than a basketball hoop!

bed

The Caterpillar 797B is the largest mechanical dump truck in the world.

LOADER

LeTourneau L-2350

Length: 62 feet (18.9 m)

Width: 22 feet, 2 inches (6.8 m)

Height: 21 feet, 2 inches (6.5 m); with bucket fully raised, 43 feet, 9 inches (13.3 m)

Weight: 270 tons (245 metric tons)

A giant dump truck needs a loader that's just as big to fill it up. The LeTourneau (*luh*-toor-NOH) L-2350 is the biggest loader in the world. With its bucket raised, it is nearly 44 feet (13.4 m) high.

A worker in the loader operates the machine's bucket, which scoops up sand or other materials and lifts it over a dump truck. The bucket then tips and drops the sand into the dump truck's bed. The L-2350 is made to lift extra-heavy loads. It can hold up to 80 tons (73 metric tons). That's like lifting more than 1,000 adults at once!

bucket

bed

loader

dump truck

The engine on the LeTourneau L-2350 is about 30 times as large as the average car engine.

HYDRAULIC SHOVEL

Terex RH 400

Length: 44 feet, 5 inches (13.5 m) **Width:** 28 feet, 3 inches (8.6 m)

Height: 32 feet, 9 inches (10 m) **Weight:** 1,078 tons (978 metric tons)

Some earthmovers are so big that they're named after dinosaurs. The world's largest hydraulic shovel is the Terex RH 400. The name of this giant machine is pronounced *T-rex*, just like the terrifying dinosaur that lived more than 65 million years ago.

A hydraulic shovel is a kind of loader. It is often used at mines to lift heavy loads of coal, rock, and sand. Liquid flows inside the machine. The liquid creates pressure that helps the shovel move and lift. The Terex RH 400 can lift 94 tons (85.3 metric tons). That's like scooping up 15 *T-rexes* at once!

T-rex

The Terex RH 400 is more than 44 feet (13.4 m) long. That's even longer than a *T-rex*, which was about 40 feet (12 m) from head to tail.

BULLDOZER

Komatsu D575A-3 Super Dozer

Length: 38 feet, 5 inches (11.7 m)   **Width:** 24 feet, 3 inches (7.4 m)

Height: 16 feet (4.9 m)   **Weight:** 168.2 tons (152.6 metric tons)

Some earthmovers just move earth. Most **bulldozers**, however, can do two jobs. They can tear up the ground and push it away.

How does a bulldozer break up the earth? There's a steel spike, called a ripper, at the back of most machines. This sharp claw can be pushed into the ground. As the bulldozer moves forward, the ripper does its ripping—easily tearing up solid rock or concrete.

The largest bulldozer in the world is the Komatsu D575A-3 Super Dozer. It doesn't have a ripper, but it does have a wide—and very powerful—blade on the front of the machine. This "dozer blade" can push about 240 tons (218 metric tons) of earth at once. That makes it strong enough to push a large airplane—as well as tear down houses, buildings, and trees that stand in its way!

ripper   tracks   blade

Komatsu D575A-3

The Komatsu D575A-3 and other bulldozers don't have tires. Instead, they move on rubber or metal tracks that help them grip the ground. The wide tracks also spread out the machines' weight so that they don't sink into the earth.

BUCKET-WHEEL EXCAVATOR

Bagger 288

Length: 705 feet (215 m)   **Weight:** 45,500 tons (41,277 metric tons)
Height: 311 feet (94.8 m)

Many kinds of earthmovers dig into the ground. The biggest of them all is a **bucket-wheel excavator** called the Bagger 288. This monster-size machine is used mostly at coal mines. It breaks up and digs out rocks and soil that cover the coal that's deep in the ground. The Bagger 288 has a giant wheel with 18 large buckets to scoop up the earth. Five people are needed to operate the huge machine, but it's worth it. In one day, it can dig up enough earth to fill a football field 98 feet (30 m) deep!

buckets

The Bagger 288 took five years to design and five more years to assemble. It cost $100 million to build the huge machine.

HYDRAULIC BREAKER

Atlas Copco HB 10000

Height of Breaker Tip:
14 feet (4.3 m)

Weight of Breaker Tip:
11 tons (10 metric tons)

Sometimes the ground at a building site is extra hard and rocky. In order to tear up the earth, a hydraulic breaker is needed. Like a hydraulic shovel, a hydraulic breaker has liquid flowing inside it. Pressure created by the liquid gives the machine the power to punch hard and fast.

The Atlas Copco HB 10000 is the most powerful hydraulic breaker in the world. The machine acts like a giant steel woodpecker. Its sharp, pointed tip punches quickly into the ground. The breaker is so strong that it can even crack concrete.

The HB 10000 strikes the ground 380 times a minute. That's more than six blows every second.

Atlas Copco HB
10000 hydraulic
breaker

TUNNEL BORER

Herrenknecht Mixshield

Length: 410 feet (125 m) **Width:** 51 feet (15.5 m)

Height: 51 feet (15.5 m) **Weight:** 2,535 tons (2,300 metric tons)

Many earthmovers dig straight down into the ground. Yet what if workers are building a tunnel? Then they need a machine that can dig across, not down. To do this, they use a **tunnel borer**. The largest kind is the Herrenknecht Mixshield. It has a giant cutting wheel that is more than 50 feet (15.2 m) high. As the borer moves forward, the wheel turns and cuts into the earth. The wheel's very sharp teeth can even cut through solid rock. Slowly, the machine carves out a long underground passage.

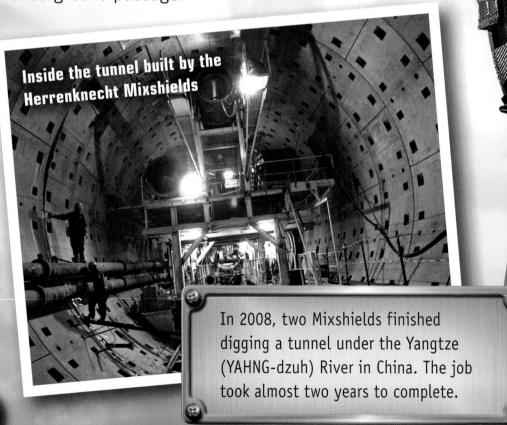

Inside the tunnel built by the Herrenknecht Mixshields

In 2008, two Mixshields finished digging a tunnel under the Yangtze (YAHNG-dzuh) River in China. The job took almost two years to complete.

質量提升質量水平　質量提升創造名牌產品

Herrenknecht Mixshield

隧道股份

MOBILE CRANE

Mammoet PTC III

Height: 656 feet (200 m)   **Weight:** 2,315 tons (2,100 metric tons)

At building sites, large lifting machines are often needed to do work in more than one place. A **mobile crane** is perfect for the job. It can lift and move anything from heavy buckets of dirt and wet concrete to long steel beams and machine equipment. The giant crane can also be driven from one place to another at a work site.

The world's biggest mobile crane is the Mammoet PTC III. Workers call it "Momo." It can turn and move in different directions. The machine has 54 wheels that allow it to even make a complete circle if necessary. Momo can lift more than 1,700 tons (1,542 metric tons). That's like lifting 300 elephants at once!

African elephant

Once Momo is no longer needed at a work site, it is taken apart and packed into 88 large containers that can then be shipped to another location.

Mammoet PTC III

BACKHOE DREDGE

Vitruvius

Length: 213 feet (65 m)   **Width:** 59 feet (18 m)

Digging Depth: 105 feet (32 m)   **Weight:** 562 tons (510 metric tons)

Most earthmovers work on dry land. A **backhoe dredge**, however, sits on a flat-bottomed boat so that it can work in water. It digs up sand and mud that has settled at the bottom of a lake, river, or ocean. A giant bucket on the backhoe dredge scoops up the muddy earth and places it on a boat called a **barge** so that it can be taken away.

The world's largest backhoe dredge is called Vitruvius. The huge machine is about 213 feet (65 m) long. Its giant bucket scoops up sand and soil that's as deep as 105 feet (32 m) in the water. When it has finished its work, the backhoe dredge, like all other huge earthmovers, is ready to begin its next giant job.

Backhoe dredges, including Vitruvius, are often used in harbors and other work areas just off the coast.

Vitruvius

bucket

MBOURG

MORE BIG EARTHMOVERS

These earthmovers are used to build roads.

First, a *scraper* prepares the ground to become a road. A blade on the bottom of the machine scrapes away bumps on the ground.

Next, a *compactor* drives along the ground to make it flat. Its heavy, metal tires smooth out the area.

After a dump truck dumps stones on the ground, they are spread around using a *grader*'s long blade.

Then, a *paver* spreads asphalt across the ground. Asphalt is a sticky material like tar that is mixed with sand and gravel.

Finally, a *roller* drives over the asphalt to make it flat. Its heavy, metal wheels make the road very smooth. When the asphalt dries, the road will be flat and hard.

GLOSSARY

backhoe dredge (BAK-hoh DREJ) a machine with a bucket that digs up sand and mud at the bottom of a lake, river, or ocean

barge (BARJ) a flat-bottomed boat that is used to carry things

bucket-wheel excavator (BUH-kit-WEEL EK-skuh-vay-tur) a machine with buckets that breaks up and digs out rocks and soil

bulldozers (BUL-*doh*-zurz) machines with a wide blade in front that moves away earth and rocks

dump truck (DUHMP TRUHK) a truck that can unload its contents by tilting the back part of its body

mine (MINE) a deep hole or tunnel from which coal and minerals, such as gold, are taken

mobile crane (MOH-buhl KRAYN) a machine with a long arm that lifts and moves heavy objects, and can be driven to different places at a work site

tunnel borer (TUHN-uhl BOR-ur) a machine that has a wheel with very sharp teeth; it is used to cut through earth and rock to build tunnels

23

INDEX

BIBLIOGRAPHY

Alves, Michael. *Heavy Equipment.* St. Paul, MN: Crestline Publishing (2003).

Haddock, Keith. *Colossal Earthmovers.* Osceola, WI: MBI Publishing (2000).

Woof, Mike. *Ultra Haulers: Global Giants of the Mining Industry.* St. Paul, MN: MBI Publishing (2006).

READ MORE

Deschamps, Nicola. *Digger.* New York: DK Publishing (2004).

MacAulay, Kelley, and Bobbie Kalman. *Cool Construction Vehicles.* New York: Crabtree Publishing (2007).

Tieck, Sara. *Earth Movers.* Edina, MN: ABDO (2005).

LEARN MORE ONLINE

To learn more about huge earthmovers, visit
www.bearportpublishing.com/WorldsBiggest

ABOUT THE AUTHOR

Meish Goldish has written more than 200 books for children.
He lives in Brooklyn, New York.